# The Christmas Book

## Jane Bull

**DK**

LONDON, NEW YORK, MUNICH,
MELBOURNE, and DELHI

DESIGN • Jane Bull
TEXT • Penelope Arlon
PHOTOGRAPHY • Andy Crawford
DESIGN ASSISTANCE • Claire Patané

MANAGING ART EDITOR • Rachael Foster
PUBLISHING MANAGER • Mary Ling
DTP DESIGNER • Almudena Díaz

For Charlotte, Billy, and James

First published in Great Britain in 2001 by
Dorling Kindersley Limited
80 Strand,
London WC2R 0RL

A Penguin Company

4 6 8 10 9 7 5

A CIP catalogue record for this book
is available from the British Library

Paperback edition ISBN: 1-4053-0151-1
Hardback edition ISBN: 0-7513-3088-4

Colour reproduction by GRB Editrice S.r.l., Verona, Italy
Printed and bound in China by Toppan

Discover more at
www.dk.com

# Christmas is coming . . .

## Christmas Countdown

## Deck the Halls

## A Feast of Pleasures

Open up No1 and begin your countdown

# Christmas Countdown

## The run up to Christmas will never be the same again with this 3-D, advent box-calendar. It'll help the days fly by!

Discover the delights in every drawer

No more boxes left to open? It must be Christmas!

# HOW TO MAKE YOUR ADVENT BOX

All you need for this spectacular advent box-calendar is one large cereal box and 23 little boxes. On the first of December open the main doors, then each day until Christmas eve open a box to reveal a surprise.

*Ask an adult . . .*
for help with the spraying

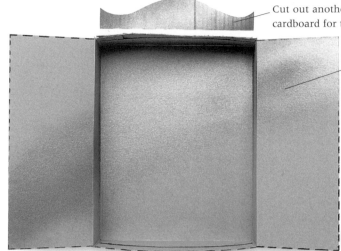

Cut out another piece of cardboard for the decorative top.

Colour the inside and outside with gold spray paint.

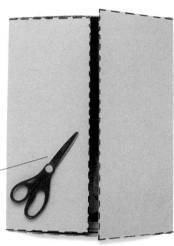

Cut down the centre of a cereal box to create doors.

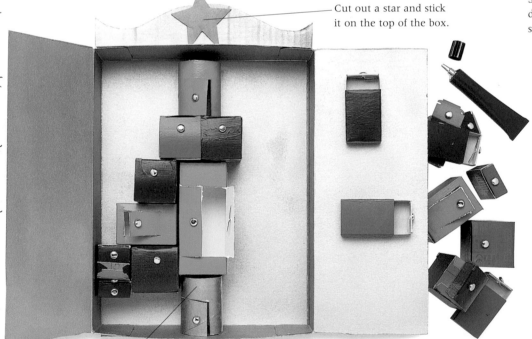

Cut out a star and stick it on the top of the box.

Stick flat boxes on the inside of the doors. Check that the calendar can shut properly.

Decorate the calendar with torn-up foil and stick a star on each little box to write the numbers on.

Glue the boxes in place – you can create any Christmas shape you like with them.

SWEET FOIL    TORN-UP FOIL    STICKERS    TREE SHAPES    PVA GLUE

6

# Collect 23 little boxes to put inside

Try out different arrangements with the boxes.

Paint the boxes with acrylic paint and PVA glue mixed together.

Cut doors in the little boxes and use split pins as handles.

Drape tinsel around the box for an extra sparkle, and decorate the star.

Tie on a card star with the number '1' on it.

## Open one box a day 'til Christmas!

Fill the boxes with goodies – sweets, jokes, messages, or toys.

Stick down small, plastic bottle tops for handles.

Tie a bow onto the doors to keep them shut.

Write the numbers, on each box inside, from 2-24.

Christmas
Greetings

# Greetings

## From the 3rd Dimension

Bouncing Rudolphs, sticking-out snowmen,
leaping stars, and a Santa bearing a bouncing gift.

They're out of this World!

Merry Christmas

Have a cracking Christmas!

# HOW TO MAKE 3-D GREETINGS

Make sure your card is the first to be noticed on the mantlepiece with these pop-up, springing, wobbling, greetings cards!

Open it up and out it pops

These templates are for the Christmas tree, the snowman, and the parcels. Cut the solid lines and fold the dotted lines. Trace them onto your folded card.

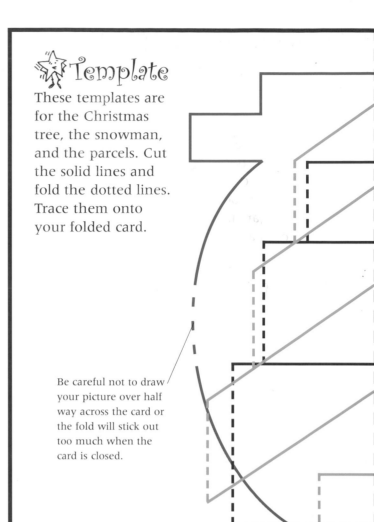

FOLD CARD HERE

Be careful not to draw your picture over half way across the card or the fold will stick out too much when the card is closed.

## ⭐ 3-D, Festive, Fold-out Card

From a flat card to a pile of presents in a Christmas flash! Four simple cuts and your greetings cards are transformed. Try the snowman and Christmas tree designs too.

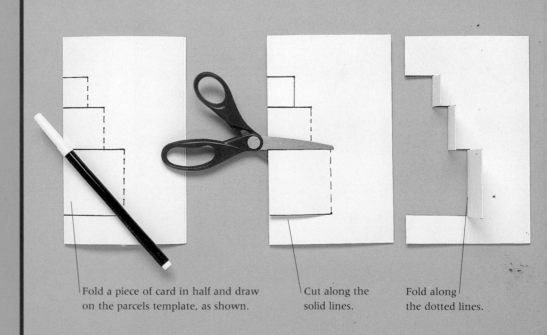

Fold a piece of card in half and draw on the parcels template, as shown.

Cut along the solid lines.

Fold along the dotted lines.

# Pop-up Wobble Card

With this magic spring card, you can make anything appear to jump out at the person who receives it – from Rudolph's nose to Santa's parcel or a twinkling star. Try out some of your own designs. How about some springing, jangling bells, or a snowman spring?

Cut out a piece of card and fold it in half.

Rudolph's nose.

Cut Rudolf's face and nose out of two other colours of card or paper. Glue the face onto the main card.

## Help Rudolph's nose wibble and wobble!

Draw a swirl on a piece of thin card – no bigger than Rudolph's nose – and cut it out.

Glue the centre of the spring to the back of the nose.

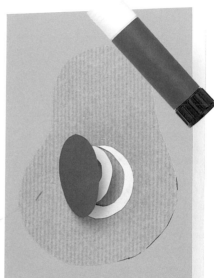

Glue the other end of the spring to Rudolph's face.

Finish Rudolph off by drawing on his features.

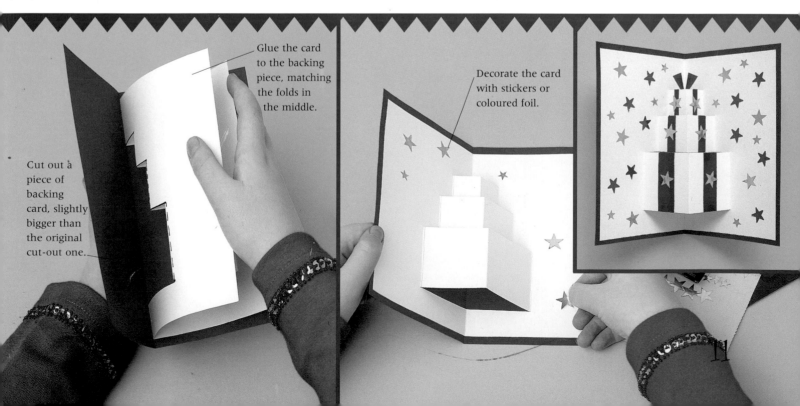

Cut out a piece of backing card, slightly bigger than the original cut-out one.

Glue the card to the backing piece, matching the folds in the middle.

Decorate the card with stickers or coloured foil.

# Paper Snow

## A flurry of paper snowflakes

float and swirl through the sky, settling in the branches of the trees.

Your paper will look like this.

Take a piece of paper and fold it in half twice along the dotted lines.

Fold it in half again.

*Snowstorms of snowflakes!*

Hang up your snowflake with cotton.

Now snip away, then unfold the flake.

*See what shapes unfold*

Get wrapped up in these paper pompoms

# BAUBLES, Orbals, and Pompoms

Baubles to hang on trees or orbals to hang on ceilings.

14

Hang out with me and my spinning baubles

Transform flat cards into shapely spheres

## ✿ Hanging Around

Glittering baubles and giant orbals swinging
and spinning around your room give it a
magical, Christmassy feel. All you need are old comics,
gift wrap, greetings cards, postcards, or anything else that's
bright – just make sure you are allowed to cut them up!

# HOW TO MAKE POMPOMS AND BAUBLES

## Paper Pompoms

Pompoms can be made out of
any paper you like. Christmas
gift wrap is jolly and bright,
or you could decorate your
own paper with a Christmas
pattern using paint or stickers.

Cut out eight discs
of paper (about
template size below).

Fold the bunch
of discs in half
and staple down
the crease.

## Baubles and Orbals

Festive baubles can be hung
on trees or simply left to spin
from ceilings. When you have
mastered the bauble, have a go
at the spectacular, giant orbal
with 20 decorated paper plates.
You'll have a task to find room
for something that big!

Take a pile of old
Christmas cards
and trace around
the template.

Cut out 20
circles, and snip
out the notches
– see template.

*Use this template to cut out 20 discs*

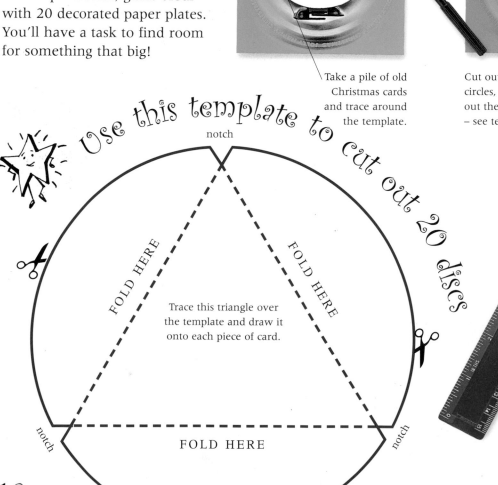

notch

FOLD HERE

FOLD HERE

Trace this triangle over
the template and draw it
onto each piece of card.

notch

FOLD HERE

notch

To help you
fold, run a
blunt-ended
pen down the
dotted lines.

16

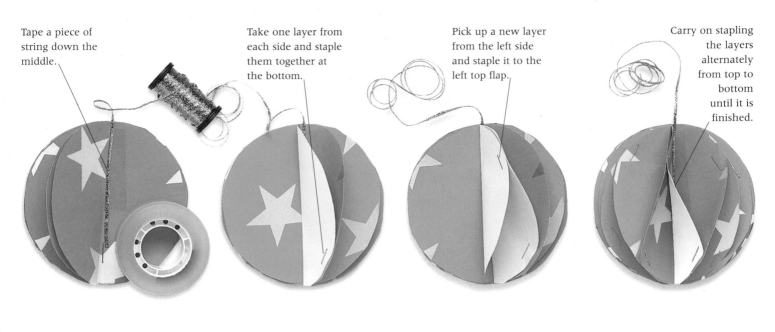

Tape a piece of string down the middle.

Take one layer from each side and staple them together at the bottom.

Pick up a new layer from the left side and staple it to the left top flap.

Carry on stapling the layers alternately from top to bottom until it is finished.

To hang up your bauble, make a hole and tie some string through it.

Staple the flaps together at each end. Keep stapling them together until they become an orb shape.

Make a giant orbal using 20 paper plates.

Wow! it's almost as big as me!

# Festoon your tree with glittering goodies

## Tree Art

There's nothing better than a tree weighed down by colourful decorations to remind you that it's Christmas. Even better if you have made them all yourself.

## Turn me into a dangling tree trinket!

## Deck the Tree

Ping-Pong angel heads, dangling Santas, glitter baubles, yoghurt pot goodie-baskets, a foil star – they look amazing and are simple to make, too.

# Christmas Tree

Turn your bedroom into a festive delight by dressing a tree with an explosion of colourful decoration.

# How to make tree decorations

## Salt Dough Dangles

300 g (10$^1/_2$ oz) plain flour
300 g (10$^1/_2$ oz) salt
200 ml (7 fl oz) water
1 teaspoon oil

Put all of the ingredients into a bowl and get stuck in.

Squeeze it together to make a ball of dough.

Cook for 20 minutes (180°C/350°F/Gas mark 4). Cool on a wire rack before painting.

Cut out shapes with a cutter or a knife.

Don't forget to make a hole in them with a cocktail stick before you cook them, so that you can hang them up.

Make a base and pinch off pieces of dough to make features.

Ask an adult . . .
to help with the oven

Delicious though they look, these decorations aren't very tasty!

---

Ho, ho, ho!

Remember the hole.

Add some string.

20    Make Santa's dough head    Build his face    Heat him up    Colour him in

# Glitter Card Dangles

All you need for these sparkling dangles is some card and lots of decoration – go wild with the sequins!

Make a hole in the top with a cocktail stick.

Thread some string through the hole.

Draw some shapes on a piece of card.

Cut the shapes out.

Glue on some coloured foil and sequins.

Add more and more sequins!

# Angel Head

Transform a cheap Ping-Pong ball into a beautiful angel's face in seconds.

Thread string through and knot at the bottom.

Make a hole at the top and bottom.

Wind string around your fingers.

Tie it in the middle.

Cut the edges.

Glue the hair to the head.

Decorate the face.

# Sweet Pots

Fill this doll-sized basket, made out of a yoghurt pot, with tasty treats.

Glue on a ribbon handle.

Decorate and fill with sweets. Yum yum!

Cut off the rim.

# Tree Top

A cardboard star smothered in glittery sweet wrappers finishes off your tree perfectly. Dress up your tree and watch that no-one steals the sweets!

Festoon your tree with lots of glitzy colours!

Torn-up foil sweet wrappers.

Glue pieces of foil onto the cardboard star.

To hang it on the tree, attach a band of card to the back with glue.

# Merry Mobiles

## Christmas is on the move.

Hang Rudolphs, Santas, Frosty snowmen, and tree faces around your room and you'll be spinning!

*Cut out shapes from cardboard and jazz them up*

Use cardboard for your mobiles.

Glitter will catch the light when the mobiles spin and give the room an extra sparkle.

*Paint the eyes*

These baubles make great tree eyes.

Ping-Pong ball eyes.

*Give the nose an extra sparkle*

Make a hole at the top and bottom, thread some string through, and knot.

22

Feeling dizzy yet?

It's melt-down for Frosty!

## ☆ In a Spin

Hang these fantastic mobiles from the ceiling and watch them spinning and twirling around. Remember to paint and decorate them on both sides so that whichever way they turn you can see exactly what they are.

# Storm in a Jam Jar

## Shake up the snow!

Catch some Christmas magic and keep it in a jar.

Wow! These sparkle more than me!

# HOW TO MAKE A SWIRLING SNOWSTORM

For your stormy winter wonderlands, all you need are some screw-top jars, water, glycerine, glitter, and a few toys. Add them together, and you'll have a perfect gift for all the movers and shakers you know!

*shake, whirl, and swirl!*

★ **Take a Jar**
Choose a small jar with a very tight, screw-top lid. You may want to test it – you don't want your snowstorms to leak everywhere.

1

*Add glitter to glycerine*

2

*Fill up with water*

3

*Give it a stir*

WATER

GLYCERINE

PLASTIC
TOY

STRONG
GLUE

GLITTER

## ✷ Glycerine

Glycerine is a non-toxic liquid that can be bought in most pharmacies. It slightly thickens the water so that your glitter-snow falls more slowly when you shake it. Use about one part glycerine to two parts water.

## ✷ Glue Tip

Use a strong glue that seals even when in water to stick down the toy. For an extra seal, add some glue inside the rim of the lid to prevent leakages.

no great shakes
they're easy
to make

Glue around the inside of the lid and the outside of the jar rim.

Decorate the lid with festive ribbon.

4

Stick down a toy

5

Pop the lid on tightly

6

Shake it up!

# Santa's on the Move

## Jingle bells! Santa's on his way. Give him a little time to fill his sleigh with goodies and he'll be up in the sky in a flash.

### Sweet Factory

All it takes to create Santa's chalet and sleigh are lots of goodies and lots of imagination. When you have built your sleigh, fill it up with bundles of bright sweets – don't be tempted to eat them – and display them on the Christmas table.

**Sugar snow sprinkled through a paper doily provides a snowy landscape for the reindeer to visit**

# How to Build Santa's Chalet and Sleigh

All you need is a piece of cardboard as the sleigh base and a milk carton for the chalet.

Biscuit layer glued down.

Cardboard base.

## Sugary Glue

Mix icing sugar and water to make a sticky paste. Spread it on with a knife and press your biscuits down on top of it.

Chocolate mini rolls and fingers.

Bars of chocolate.

Cut off the bottom of the carton if it is too tall.

Paste on chocolate fingers as logs for the house.

A biscuit makes a good front to start building on.

## Sticky Tip

If your roof keeps slipping down, pop the box into the fridge for a few minutes to let the icing harden.

**Candy canes for speedy runners**

Remember to leave enough room on the base for the runners.

A biscuit for Santa to rest his back on.

Jelly beans and hard gums are great for decoration.

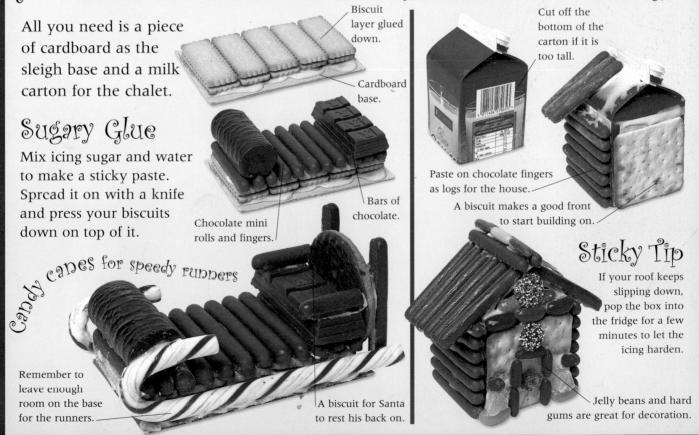

# A Winter Wonderland

## Who would ever know

that these Christmassy characters in their wintery lands are more than just great-looking faces? Open them and see for yourself.

Hats off to penguins with presents!

Keep your head or you'll give away the secret!

★ Goodies Galore
Don't just build one snowman, make a whole family to guard the presents and keep extra presents safely inside. Create a forest of trees in a snowy land, filled to the brim with gifts and goodies.

The penguin and snowman chat happily, keeping their secrets under their hats!

# How to make gift boxes

Collect all sorts of tubes, big or small, fat or thin, from crisp boxes and biscuit tubes to toilet and kitchen rolls – all are perfect for your character boxes. The important thing is to fill them with sweets, or other little gifts, and surprise someone on Christmas Day.

## Penguin Box

A large tube is perfect for making a performing penguin. When you have mastered the fiddly bits, why not try making some smaller penguin chicks?

Cut off a third of the way down the tube.

Make a card band and wrap it neatly inside the top part. This will keep the lid on.

Cut out two wings from a piece of card.

Glue the band into place.

Measure a good sized beak to stick onto the head.

Wing.

Cut out a penguin tail and two flappy feet.

Tape the features to the tube.

## Festive Firs

Hang these trees up by their ribbons or sit them in a foresty line-up. Why not put them around the base of a Christmas tree?

Cut a semi-circle of paper to make a cone big enough for your container.

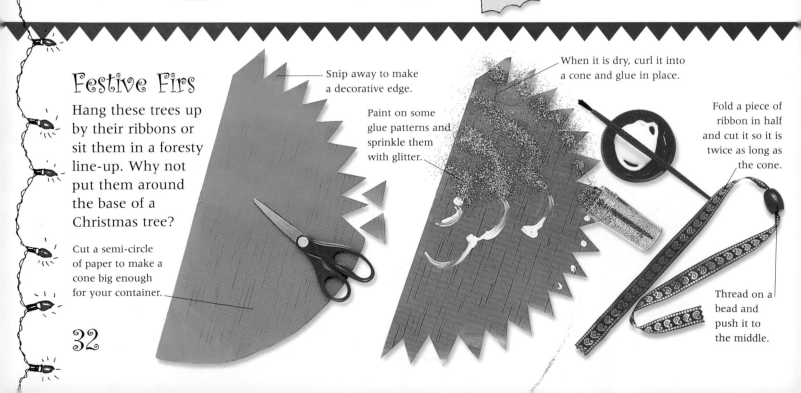

Snip away to make a decorative edge.

Paint on some glue patterns and sprinkle them with glitter.

When it is dry, curl it into a cone and glue in place.

Fold a piece of ribbon in half and cut it so it is twice as long as the cone.

Thread on a bead and push it to the middle.

32

# Penguin Suit

Put glue along the edge.

Cut out a triangle of material.

Make this edge long enough to fit around the top of the head with a 5 mm (¹/4 in) overlap.

Try it on your penguin and trim it until it fits. Glue the sides together.

Glue the hat to the tube.

Add a band and a bobble.

Give him some eyes.

Make clothes out of scraps of material.

Paint the penguin with acrylic paint and PVA glue mixed together.

Paint the features using different colours.

*Now fill up your penguin!*

# Dressing the Snowman

Prepare a tube in the same way as the penguin box.

Tape on pipe cleaner arms.

Spread glue on the box and cover it with tufts of cotton wool.

Put a ribbon through the lid and tape it in place.

Try making a junior snowman with a small tube.

Decorate him with material scraps.

Cover a container with gift wrap for the trunk of the tree.

Make a small hole in the top and thread the ribbon through it.

Pierce two holes in the container and tie the two ribbon ends through them.

Pop on the lid to keep the goodies locked up.

*A forest of firs . . .*

*. . . filled with fancies*

33

# Host of Angels

**Heavenly biscuits** adorn the table during the Christmas feast and angelic paper plates flutter gracefully around the sparkling Christmas tree.

## Angel Food

250 g (9 oz) plain flour
125 g (4$^1$/$_2$ oz) butter
60 g (2 oz) caster sugar

Put all of the ingredients into a bowl and rub them together with your fingers to make crumbs. Slowly knead together to make a ball.

Cook for 10-15 mins (160°C/320°F/ Gas mark 3).

Crush boiled sweets and put them into the centre before you cook them for a stained glass look.

Roll out the pastry to about 1 cm ($^1$/$_3$ in) thick.

Cut a template out of card and use it to cut out the shapes.

Cut a hole in the centre of the angels.

Use cocktail sticks to make patterns.

Silver sugar balls are great for extra decoration.

Cut out the shape

Staple the skirt

Decorate the angel

# Flying Angels

A host of cherubs and angels float
dreamily through the sky on
Christmas night. Attach
a piece of string to the
paper angels so that you can
hang them up on branches. Let
the heavenly biscuits cool and
delight your family with
your celestial snacks.

# Santa's Sweet Factory

Yum Yum

## Ho, ho, ho, Santa's been busy rustling up some tasty truffles to tickle the tastebuds.

Ask an adult . . .
to melt the butter

### ⭐ Rudolf's Truffles

125 g (4¹/2 oz) melted butter
250 g (9 oz) crushed digestive biscuits
4 tablespoons coconut
4 tablespoons cocoa
4 tablespoons honey

Crush the biscuits in a bag

Mix all the ingredients together in the pan

### ⭐ Easy Peasy

The best thing about the truffles is that once the butter has melted there's no more cooking. Ask an adult to melt the butter while you crush the biscuits. Let the pan cool before you add the rest of the ingredients.

Wash your hands . . .
before you touch the mixture

Pour the mixture into a tray

Divide the mixture into squares with a knife.

Place the tray into a fridge for a few hours.

Roll the squares into balls

# Magic Marzipan

To make truffle Santas, mix some drops of food colouring into a little marzipan, and squash into Santa's features. Shape some holly leaves and berries as decoration for the plate.

*Squeeze, roll, and squash into Santa's features*

*Cover your truffles with delicious decoration*

*Coconut, chopped nuts, cocoa, or grated chocolate – anything you can think of!*

Roll the truffles and pop them into a paper case.

# Frosty Welcomes

**Light up the night** before Christmas with shining ice decorations or glistening ice-bowl lanterns.

## They're illuminating!

Make your garden glow
with Christmassy candlelight

A welcome glow for festive friends

# HOW DOES YOUR GARDEN GLOW?

All you need for a Christmas glow is some seasonal cuttings, candles, and lots of ice. You can use anything wintery for your foliage, from holly and ivy to rosehips and cranberries – just get outside, get picking, and create a welcoming light outside in your garden.

## ⭐ The Big Freeze

Position a small bowl inside a larger one and tape it so that it is hanging in the centre – not touching the bottom or sides. Fill it with foliage and water, and freeze it.

If the small bowl bobs up too much, put some pebbles in it to weigh it down.

## ⭐ Defrost Tip

To remove the bowls, you may have to dip the frozen lantern in warm water, and pour a little into the smaller bowl as well, to loosen the ice.

## ⭐ Ice Light

Use half a plastic bottle and a cup for the long lanterns, making sure that the cup doesn't touch the edges of the bottle at all. Use small or tall candles for the inside and if it starts to defrost, perk it up by putting it back into the freezer for a while.

## Ask an adult...

⭐ to light the candles

1

Fill the containers

2

Drop in the plants

# Let it all hang out in the garden

Tape the string to the sides of the lid to stop it from moving while it freezes.

## ✨ Ice Art

Find a lid or a tray with at least a 1 cm (¹/2 in) tall rim and fill it with water. Put your plant decorations into it then drape the ends of a long piece of string in either side – they will freeze with the ice and can be used to hang it up.

Fill up with water

4

Freeze it all up

5

Let it glow

Find a box your size

and ask an adult . . .

to cut three holes in it
for your arms and head

# Pass the Parcel

Do you have a
Christmas hat?
If so, put it on!

Decorate a hair
band with tinsel
for an extra
sparkle.

If you can fit your
whole body into the
box, it makes a very
cunning disguise.

42

Finish off
your outfit
by carrying
another
parcel – you
could fill it
with goodies.

# All you need is a cardboard box to create a parcel party-piece to parade around in!

## Wrap it Up

When you have your arm and head holes, simply wrap up the box using a roll of gift wrap and sticky tape.

## Ribbons and Bows

To make ribbons and bows, cut long strips of paper and tape them around the box. Fold some extra strips into bow shapes and tape into position.

If you find a big enough box, keep your head inside and make a peep hole at the front.

Why not wear a red Christmas outfit underneath your box?

43

# That's Entertainment!

**Family and friends** like nothing more than to sit back, relax, and be entertained. So spoil them with a spectacular show.

## You're a Star

### Abracadabra!

#### Hey Presto!

Know any magic tricks? If so, then create a magician's costume and astonish your audience. If not, then tell a few jokes or a made-up story.

## I'll sing you a song

### A Bit of a Song and Dance

Sing a few old favourites and encourage the audience to join in, or try your hand at one of the latest songs in the charts. When you have perfected the music, put a dance routine to it.

## Carol singers

There's nothing better at Christmas than a good sing-along of the carols that everyone knows. Perform them at home or persuade an adult to take you out on a tour of the neighbourhood. You could collect money for a charity of your choice.

## Hark the Herald Angels Sing . . .

# What a Performance!

## ⭐ Curtains Up!

Perform a play to your family
and friends using various props and costumes.
Try a puppet show using some old socks.

## A round of applause for . . .

### ⭐ That's Show Business!

Making costumes is easier than you think, all you have
to do is search around your house for odds and ends and
use your imagination. You can create a pantomime horse
with a rug and a cardboard box, or a fairy with a ballet
outfit and a few home-made props. Invent your own
story or simply use an old favourite.

## Hocus pocus, turn into a horse!

# Welcome to the Christmas Quiz

Try hosting a game show for
your family. Invent your
own catch-phrases and give
away prizes – tempt the
contestants with them at the
beginning of the show. Make
up some questions or simply
ask them to race each other
with simple tasks.

## Take your seats please

### The Christmas Show

Performed by:
The Festive players

Act One: Aunty Jane arrives
Act Two: Disaster Dessert
Interval
Act Three: Jamie saves the day!
Grand Finale

Draw your own programme
for a show. Why not pretend
to be members of your family
and act out a family scene. Be
careful not to upset anyone!

# Packing Presents

**It's the night** before Christmas and as dusk falls stockings are waiting to be filled through the night. So surprise Santa with these bright ones!

Attach a tag to the top so that you can hang it up.

Stick all of the decorations on with a fabric glue. It will say on the tube if it is suitable.

Cut out two sock shapes and stick them together with a fabric glue.

*Make them big, Santa's stuffing more in this year!*

Cut Rudolph's face shape out of felt and stick it to the stocking. Use different colours for the features.

## A Stitch in Time

To jazz up the stocking, try your hand at blanket stitch around the edges.

Start the stitch by putting the needle through about 1 cm (¹/₂ in) away from the edge.

Bring the thread under the needle as you pull it down and through – it's as simple as that!

Fill me up to the brim

Stick 'em Up!

If the stockings are ready then it's almost Christmas Day. Hurray! Hang it up and wait for Santa, or you could make one as a gift for someone special.

These felt snowflakes prove that you don't have to use a lot of colours to get a great Christmas look.

The best thing about these stockings is that you can use them year after year.

# INDEX

# ACKNOWLEDGEMENTS

With additional thanks to . . .
Maisie Armah, Charlotte Bull, Billy Bull, James Bull, Sorcha Lyons, and Kailen Wilcox for being merry models.
Additional photography:
Dave King for the magician page 44, the fairy and the pantomime horse page 45
Steve Shott for the carol singers page 39, 44